DATE DUE

NOV. 1	2-5		
OCT 2 8 1980			
		DISCARDED	

B   Braun
Wilson   On stage Flip Wilson

4.95x   c.1

text
Thomas Braun

design concept
Larry Soule

photos
Globe: pp. 6, 20, 42
UPI: pp. 8, 10, 16, 22, 30, 36, 40

published by
Creative Education,
Mankato, Minnesota

ON STAGE
FLIP WILSON

WOODSIDE ELEM

Published by Creative Educational Society, Inc.,
123 South Broad Street, Mankato, Minnesota 56001
Copyright ® 1976 by Creative Educational Society, Inc. International
copyrights reserved in all countries.
No part of this book may be reproduced in any form without written
permission from the publisher. Printed in the United States.
Distributed by
Childrens Press, 1224 West Van Buren Street, Chicago, Illinois 60607

Library of Congress Numbers: 75-425-06   ISBN: 0-87191-489-1

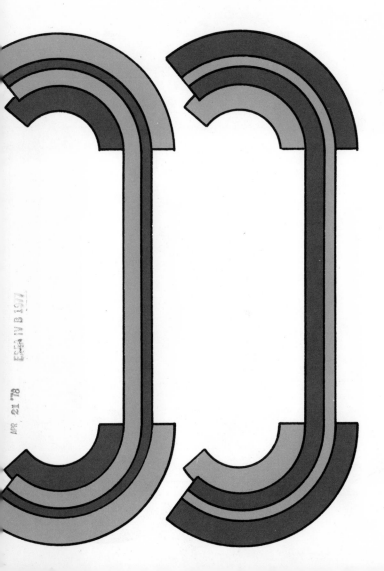

5

"Cleeeeeeerow!" shouted Miss Davis. "Clerow, stop that. You're supposed to be a wounded soldier." Clerow Wilson was trying to make his small part in the school play just a little bit bigger. No, actually, he was trying to make his part a lot bigger. First he pretended to be wounded in the leg, then in the stomach, then in the head. He played dead, stood up and died again. He struggled to his knees, whispered "that's all folks" and collapsed a third time. The other students in the play were collapsing too, from laughter. But not Miss Davis.

"I'm just trying to see what it really feels like to get wounded," apologized Clerow.

"Clerow, can you see my right hand," Miss Davis smiled calmly. "Can you see, Clerow, how quickly I can change this gentle old hand into a big powerful fist . . . like this?"

"You know, Miss Davis," Clerow nodded, "I think I just figured out how you want me to play this part. So if you don't mind, I guess I'll just lie down here and moan very, very quietly." With a few snickers, the rehearsal continued.

The students in Miss Davis's room at P.S. 14 were working on a production of **Clara Barton,**

Red Cross Nurse. The school in Jersey City, New Jersey, needed to raise money for band uniforms. Miss Davis and her class had volunteered to help by staging a play.

The play was about the famous nurse who treated wounded soldiers on the battlefields during the Civil War and who later founded the American Red Cross.

The day before the play was to be performed, Miss Davis stood in front of her class. Her face showed that something was wrong. Miss Davis told the class that the girl who played the part of Clara Barton was sick. She had the measles and couldn't possibly recover in time for the performance. Miss Davis shook her head and the class groaned. Without the lead actress, without someone to play Clara Barton, the play was finished.

Clerow Wilson raised his hand. "This is no time for smart remarks," the teacher cautioned.

"No, Maam," Clerow said, "I have a very serious suggestion." He emphasized the word "serious" and quickly added, "I can do the part." First there was silence, then the class groaned even louder than before. As Miss Davis was about to raise her gentle hand once more, Clerow started reciting Clara Barton's lines. He remembered them perfectly. He knew every one of the lines. Miss Davis thought for a moment and then suggested a vote, "All in favor of letting Clerow

Wilson play the part of Clara Barton, raise your hands." Clerow's hand shot up first. Then a few other hands joined his. Finally, even the most skeptical students indicated their consent.

"Hey, Clara, I've got a mean stomach-ache," someone joked.

"Just learn your lines, chump," Clerow replied, " 'cause if you don't, this little nurse is gonna operate on your skull."

Miss Davis restored order and turned her class's attention to multiplication.

No one remembers much about Clerow Wilson's first performance on the school stage in Jersey City. He may have tried hard to be serious, but even Miss Davis must have laughed. Later, the animated TV version of Clara Barton left no doubt that Clerow Wilson made his mark.

One thing is certain. This wasn't the only time in his life that Clerow would dress up like a woman and make people laugh. Long after **Clara Barton, Red Cross Nurse,** Clerow changed his first name to "Flip." He exchanged the white nurse's cap and apron for a long brown wig and false eyelashes. Clara became Geraldine. And what we saw was what we got: Flip Wilson became the most successful black comedian in the history of television.

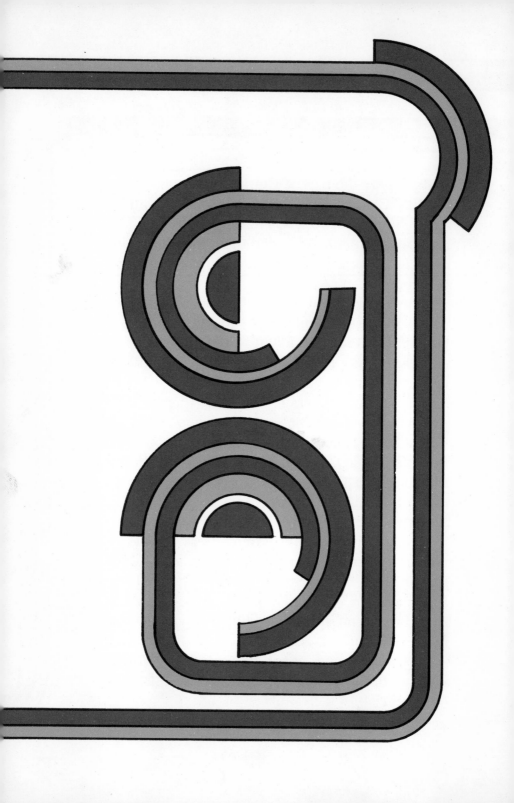

brothers
and
sisters

Flip Wilson never talks much about his childhood. Comedians tell stories to make people laugh. And the story of Flip's early years isn't very funny.

Flip was born in 1933. His mother and father and his seventeen brothers and sisters lived in a poor black neighborhood in Jersey City, New Jersey. "We were so poor," he recalls, "that even the poor people on our block looked down on us." When Flip was five years old his mother deserted her family. With his wife gone, Flip's father was left with the impossible task of feeding and caring for his hungry children. Flip's father worked part-time as a janitor in the stores along Jackson Avenue. He tried to find extra work as a carpenter. A neighbor remembers Mr. Wilson standing on the street corner with his hammer and saw waiting for someone to walk by and offer him a job.

Flip's father tried desperately to keep his many sons and daughters together. The huge family constantly moved from place to place searching for the cheapest possible rent. Their most miserable home was a cold basement room which father and children shared with a large pile of coal. With barely enough money to afford shelter, there was little left over to buy food. In order to survive, Flip's brothers and sisters were forced to take food from a nearby supermarket.

The situation grew worse. Reluctantly, Mr. Wilson agreed to have all of his children placed in foster homes. The only alternative was starvation.

Flip's first foster mother was only interested in the welfare money she received for caring for Flip and one of his brothers. She refused to allow any contact between Flip and her own son. She forced the brothers to stay out of sight in a small, unfinished room above the kitchen.

When Flip's brother was sent to reform school at Whitesboro, New Jersey, Flip wanted to go there too. He ran away from his foster home seven times. "Anytime the situation got shaky, I split." He split again, and after the eighth attempt, he succeeded. The seven-year-old boy was sent to join his brother at Whitesboro.

For most people, reform school is an unhappy place. But not for Flip. For the first time, he was given decent clothes and enough food to eat. He ate so much that his friends nick-named him, "Tin Can." Life was much better at Whitesboro than it had ever been in Jersey City. Flip made several clumsy escape attempts in order to extend his stay. He knew that each time he was caught his stay would be extended. Not only was his stomach full, but he also met people who seemed to care for him. Every night one of the guards saved his dessert and gave it to Flip. On his eighth birthday, that same guard and his wife gave Flip a box of Crackerjacks and a can of ABC Shoe Polish. Not much, perhaps, but it was the first birthday present that Flip had ever received. Others cared too. Mrs. Jones, a teacher at the school, moved Flip ahead into a class of students his own age. He worked hard to prove to her that he was as intelligent as she thought he was.

class-clown

Flip left reform school and was returned to Jersey City. He moved from one foster home to another. Again he felt lost and hungry. Yet even during these early difficult years, circumstances began to shape his later career.

Flip remembers sneaking into the old Mosque Theatre to see the stars of vaudeville. He enjoyed the singers, the dancers and the acrobatic acts. But his favorite performers were the comedians. Flip had always been able to make people laugh. He played the class-clown in school. He liked to trade funny stories with the firemen outside the corner fire station. Jokes came easily for the skinny boy. He was never big enough to fight his way out of an argument. But the right words thrown in at the right time, left opponents too weak to fight. Sometimes he'd annihilate his opponent with a line like this:

"Hold it! Now you're gonna hit me, right? O.K., but I gotta tell you this first. If you hit me real hard, see, I'll probably fall right down, plop! Right down here on the ground, like this. See, this is where I'll be. Now when I do fall right down here on the ground . . . after you hit me . . . 'cause you're so mad . . . you are mad, aren't you? Anyway, my big dog Buster — the one over there hiding behind that bench — my big dog Buster is

17

going to walk over here very slowly. He's going to sniff at me lying here on the ground. He'll look at you, look down at me and he'll say: 'Roll over, dummy.' Now I don't mind if you hit me, but it sure is going to hurt my feelings when Buster talks to me that way."

By the time Flip finished his story, everybody was laughing and all the anger had disappeared. Flip learned early that to be funny was to be powerful. He listened carefully to the black comedians at the Mosque Theatre. He heard them make audiences laugh at jokes about the miseries of being poor and black. The comedians had the magic to make people happy and, even more important, they got paid for it. As Flip listened to the applause, he knew he had the magic. He knew what he wanted to be.

Another influence on his future career came from one of his many foster homes. For a short time he and his brother lived with a family whose religious convictions were very strong. The family forbade the boys to see movies or listen to the radio or read comic books. Without these kinds of entertainments, Flip would lie awake at night and make-up his own stories to amuse his brother.

"Remember when Daddy gave me that pair of sister's shoes with the heels cut off?" Flip might say and then ramble on with a story like this: "Well, I was walking down the street one day, carrying this big sack of money to the bank, and some guy stops me and says, 'Where'd you get them dumb lookin' shoes from?' Well, I set down my big sack of money and said to the man, 'These shoes may look dumb to you, Jack, but they cost me forty dollars.' 'Forty dollars for a pair of shoes?' the man said. 'No,' I said, 'forty dollars for the right one. The left one belongs to my sister.' "

And then there was Geraldine. Flip tells this story: a nine-year old West Indian girl named Geraldine lived on his block. Geraldine promised she would be Flip's girl-friend if he would buy her a pair of false-fingernails. When he told her that he didn't have any money, she told him, "Honey, if you really care for Geraldine, your own fingers will figure out a way to get 'em." Flip got the message and got the fingernails. When he returned to her house, he found that he had grabbed the wrong size. Back to the store he went. This time he took the right size, but Geraldine still wasn't happy. She wanted a pair for her sister. He returned to the store a third time, but got caught. The manager threatened to call the police, then pushed the frightened boy out the front door. When Flip told his story to Geraldine, she refused to speak to him. "Because, honey, I never talk to criminals." Flip didn't get the girl, but he tucked her name away for future use.

kitchen
clown

Forced to choose between money and education, Flip dropped out of high school. He worked briefly on a construction project then picked up odd jobs in a bowling alley and a parking lot. In 1949, when he was 16 years old, he persuaded a recruiting officer that he was really 18 and joined the Air Force. Like reform school, the Air Force offered him much more comfort and security than the streets of Jersey City. He received new clothes, medical care and $100 every month.

His first assignment was kitchen duty. The class-clown became the kitchen-clown. He entertained the men in the mess hall with his imitations. Sometimes he borrowed the language of Shakespeare so that some well-known speeches might sound like this:

"Friends, Romans, Aviators, lend me your trays/I come to wash your dishes not to break them/The food that men leave, fills garbage cans/Some spoons are oft interred with the bones.

"The quality of garbage is not strained/It droppeth as the gentle rain from heaven/Upon my shoes beneath."

21

One day one of the cooks responded to Flip's performance, "Me thinks King Clerow hath flippeth his lid." The word "Flippeth" got shortened to "flip" and the name stuck. Flip had never liked the name "Clerow." He was happy to give it up.

Flip was shipped to Guam. There his comic talents became famous. He was ordered to tour Air Force bases in the Pacific and perform for the troops. Flip would tailor his jokes to suit Air Force life.

"I met this pilot the other day who was afraid of heights. He didn't mind flying so much, but he hated sleeping in the top bunk. No one knew he was scared of heights until one night somebody noticed he slept with his parachute on. Poor guy missed breakfast every morning, 'cause after he bailed out of bed, it took him an hour to fold up his 'chute."

The Air Force gave Flip his first opportunity to stand up in front of a large audience and be funny. Like the pilot in the top bunk, Flip's career as a comedian was just barely off the ground.

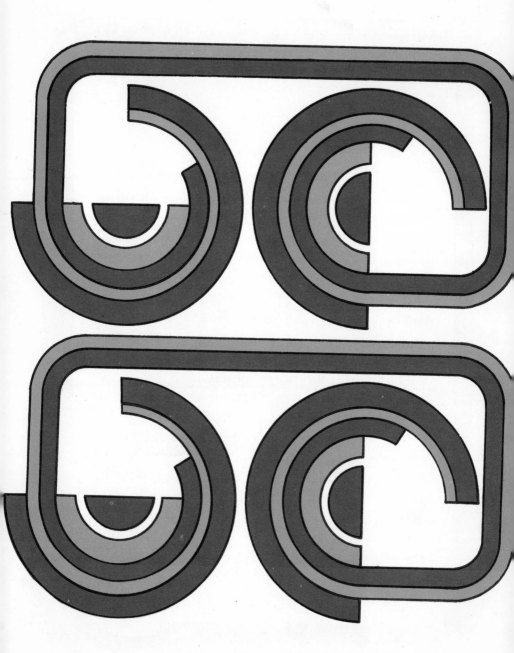

cross country

In 1954, Flip faced an important decision. He could re-enlist in the Air Force, or he could give up the economic security of military life and try to make it as a professional comedian. Flip had read stories about famous people in show business. Most of them had worked hard for 15 years before achieving success. He was determined to follow the same 15-year schedule. He was discharged from the Air Force and moved to San Francisco.

Flip took a job as a bell-hop at the Manor Plaza Hotel and carried suitcases for $40 a week. Members of a dance act in the hotel's nightclub asked Flip to tell some jokes one night while they changed their costumes. His short routine was so successful that the dancers invited Flip to join their tour of California. The first stop was a hotel in Stockton where Flip received 95¢ for each of his performances. At the same time he was paying the hotel $2 a night for his room. The Stockton engagement lasted nine months and Flip's nightly salary increased to $7.

Flip left California and started a long cross-country journey. Constantly searching for places

to perform, he hitchhiked from town to town. When his money ran out, he slept outside under a tree or in a bus station or even on the top of a parked car. He performed in small-town bars and nightclubs. He made barely enough money to move on to another club and another bus station. Flip spent every free minute re-working old stories and writing new material for his act. By this time he had become a serious student of comedy. When a joke didn't work, when it got silent stares instead of loud laughs, Flip wanted to know why. He changed words. He changed timing. No story was right until it made people laugh. For several long years Flip was hungry again, but he was also becoming a better comedian. The goal of his 15-year plan kept him going.

One night in 1959, Flip was playing a small nightclub in Miami, Florida. A man named Herbie Shul listened to the young comedian and was impressed. After Flip finished his act, Shul approached him. "What's your biggest problem?" Shul asked. "Money, of course, and a place to sleep," Flip said. Then Herbie Shul made Flip a surprising offer. He said he'd give him $50 every week for a year, if Flip would concentrate on perfecting his material. "If you make it to the top, you can return the money. If you don't, well, you can just forget it." For Shul, the money was an investment. For Flip the money meant time to concentrate on comedy instead of survival. And

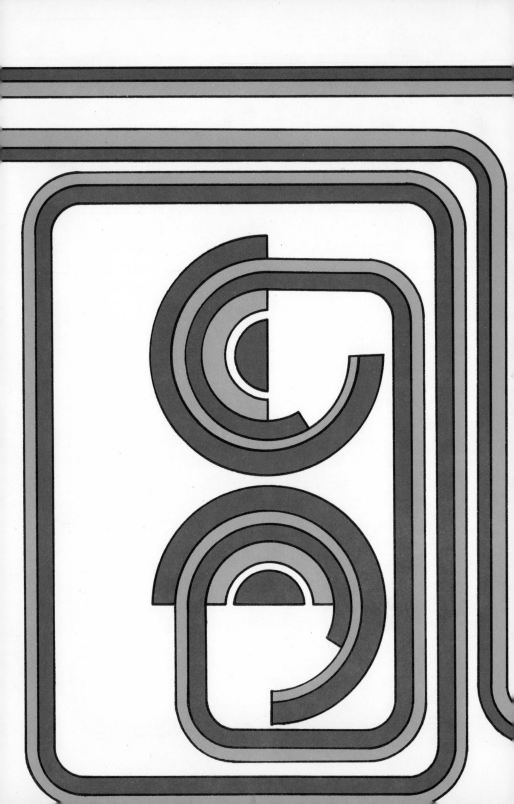

that was exactly the kind of break he needed. He agreed to take the money. He got even more serious about being funny.

During this period, Flip developed several new routines and created new comic characters. With both new material and new confidence, Flip was able to find jobs at some of the top black theaters in the country. He left the small-town bars behind and performed in big theaters like the Regal in Chicago, and the Howard in Washington, D.C. He played on the most important stage for all black entertainers: the Apollo Theater in Harlem, New York.

At the Apollo, Flip met Monte Kay, the manager of several musical groups who appeared at the Harlem theater. After numerous long discussions about the young comedian's career, Monte Kay agreed to become Flip's manager. It had been 10 years since Flip had been discharged from the Air Force. He was pleased with his own progress, but not content. In order to achieve the kind of success that he wanted, he knew he needed to reach a larger audience.

tonight
show

In the summer of 1965, the popular black comedian, Redd Foxx, appeared on the **Tonight Show.** The host of the television program, Johnny Carson, asked Redd about his favorite comedians. Without hesitating, Redd said that the best new comedian was Flip Wilson. To Johnny Carson and the millions of people watching the show, the name Flip Wilson meant nothing. But Johnny's curiosity and interest in helping new talent would change all that. With instructions from the host, the **Tonight Show** talent coordinator contacted Monte Kay. The date for Flip's first television appearance was quickly set.

Flip arrived at the NBC television center two hours before the show was scheduled to begin. He was given a quick tour of the studio. Like almost every other American, Flip had watched the **Tonight Show** many times. The stage on which he would perform appeared much smaller than he had imagined. It was dark and cluttered and, for Flip, painfully silent. Flip wondered, when the rows of empty seats were filled, when

31

he faced the studio audience and the TV cameras, would he find the same silence? "Just learn your lines, chump, 'cause if you don't, this little nurse is gonna operate on your skull." Performing on the **Tonight Show** couldn't be more difficult than playing Clara Barton at P.S. 14. Could it?

As Flip was led to his dressing room, he passed an open door. Inside the small room, he spotted a make-up man patiently working over Johnny Carson. The show's host and the producer were calmly discussing details of the program.

Just as Flip finished dressing, the talent coordinator arrived and ushered him to a larger waiting room. "Do your best. Remember, ten million people will be watching." The coordinator's quiet words and gentle smile hit Flip like a very large hammer. He found an empty spot on a long vinyl couch and stared at the television monitor in the corner. Ten million people . . . ten million relaxed, sleepy people. Flip shook off the tension and listened for the sound of ten million people laughing.

Of course Flip was nervous. But he knew that in five minutes on the **Tonight Show** he would reach more people than the combined total of all his previous audiences. He had been rehearsing for more than ten years. He could be good for five minutes. Many of the country's top entertainers had been "discovered" on the **Tonight Show:** Andy Williams, Dick Gregory, Carol Burnett, Nipsey Russell, Joan Rivers, Barbra Streisand and Bill Cosby. Flip promised himself that he would be next.

"You're next," someone called. Flip looked up and saw that the words were directed toward him. He smiled. "Just like the dentist's office," he thought to himself. Again he was being led through a narrow corridor and into the studio. Flip waited behind a curtain. He could hear Johnny Carson talking casually with someone in the audience. The rest of the country was watching commercials for dog food, shampoo and aspirin. Suddenly, the studio was quiet and Johnny was announcing his next guest. The brief introduction was followed by polite applause. The band played something, a stagehand held

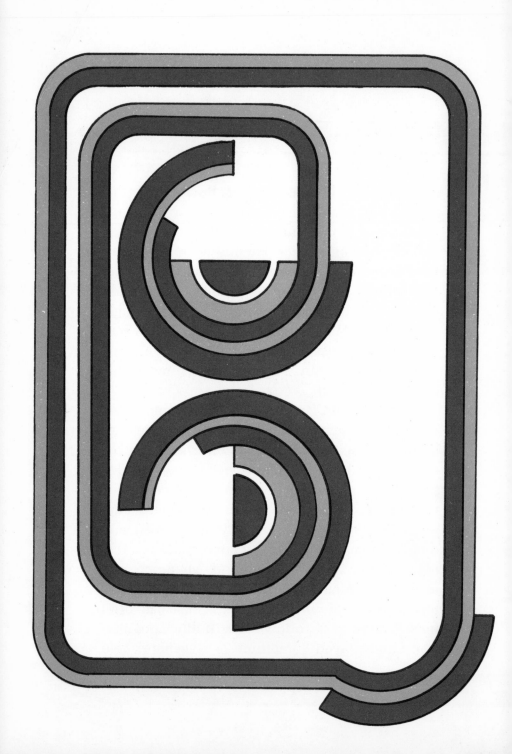

the curtain open and Flip made the most important entrance of his career.

"Hello, my name's Flip Wilson. A few weeks ago I was riding this train between New York and Washington. I got settled and glanced across the aisle. There was a woman holding a baby. Generally, I'd be reluctant to express an opinion about a kid, but this was a really ugly baby . . . **bad** looking baby. I know an ugly baby when I see one. This fellow enters the coach and he stops and stares at the baby. 'What do you think you're looking at?' the woman asks. 'I'm just looking at your ugly baby, lady,' the man says. 'I bet you save a lot of money with that baby. You don't have to hire a baby sitter, no one's going to bother that kid.' Naturally, the woman took offense at this. She called the conductor and complained that the man was bothering her. 'I'm sorry,' the conductor apologized. 'To make it up to you, maam, we'll give you a free lunch. And maybe I can even find a banana for your monkey.' "

Every story that Flip told got bigger and bigger laughs. No one laughed harder than Johnny Carson. Flip finished his routine and the audience roared its approval. In five short minutes, the unknown comedian had stepped into a new world. Television had become Flip's frontier. He was eager to conquer the new wilderness.

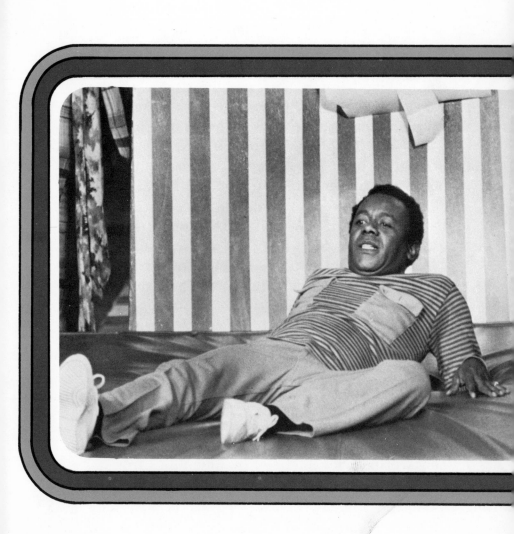

on schedule

In the weeks that followed his first television appearance, Flip was flooded with offers and requests. Television has a big appetite for new talent and, almost overnight, television developed a taste for Flip. He returned four times to perform on the **Tonight Show.** During the next few years he accepted invitations from Ed Sullivan, Joey Bishop, Merv Griffin, Carol Burnett and Dean Martin. He appeared frequently on Rowan and Martin's **Laugh-In.** Television had boosted Flip's weekly salary from $350 to $5,000. In May, 1968, he signed a five-year exclusive contract with NBC. Three separate times the following year he was a week-long substitute host on the **Tonight Show.**

In addition to television appearances, Flip was playing college concerts, top nightclubs and the big Las Vegas hotels. He made his first comedy record album in 1967 and two more the next year. In the fall of 1969 — exactly 15 years after he had left the Air Force — NBC scheduled the first **Flip Wilson Special.**

Flip and the show's producer, Bob Henry, made careful plans. They invited Jonathan Winters to be Flip's guest. Flip also decided the up-coming program would be the right place to introduce something new.

After years of study, he had developed a new comic character. He had often used a high, sassy female voice in his routines. In his famous sketch about Christopher Columbus, Flip portrayed the Queen of Spain — Queen Isabel Johnson — with a thoroughly ethnic screech. As the explorer's ships departed, the Queen hollered after him, "Chris goin' to America on that boat. Chris goin' to find Ray Charles." In Flip's own version of a biblical story, Bathsheba swooned to the music of Little David, "play on the harp, Little David, play on that harp, honey."

On the **Flip Wilson Special,** the same distinctive voice emerged again. But this time the shrill sound was part of a complete character — Flip's most famous funny lady — Geraldine.

With the help of Geraldine, Flip's first "special" was a smash hit. Of all the people watching television that night, 42 per cent watched Flip. The show ranked eighth in the weekly ratings. These impressive statistics convinced the NBC program officials that Flip was capable of more than occasional guest appearances on television. They considered the possibility of giving Flip his own weekly show.

The format for the proposed weekly series was a problem. NBC was skeptical of the comedy-variety format. No black entertainer had ever hosted a successful variety series. Both Leslie Uggams and Sammy Davis Jr. had tried and failed. Some of the most famous people in show business — superstars like Jerry Lewis, Judy Garland, and Frank Sinatra — had also failed as variety hosts. Someone suggested a half-hour situation comedy series in which Flip might play a disc jockey or a TV talk-show host. But Flip and his manager rejected that possibility. Finally NBC agreed to gamble on the variety show format.

The **Flip Wilson Show** began in September, 1970. In its first week it became the top-ranked show on television. And throughout the entire first season, it consistently ranked among the top-ten programs. The huge success of Flip's show was reflected in the amounts of money sponsors agreed to pay in order to sell their products. When the series began, sponsors paid $45,000 for a one-minute commercial. Two months later the price increased to $65,000. In the show's third season, the same one-minute had an $86,000 price tag. NBC had gambled on Flip and won. Flip Wilson had become the most popular comedian on television.

study and perfection

Flip Wilson's rapid climb from the **Tonight Show** to his own weekly series can be partially explained by the power and mass appeal of television itself. But a television camera can only communicate what it sees. When the camera points at Flip, it sees a small, round-faced man whose warmth and easy humor invite friendly attention. What the camera may not pick up is the seriousness which Flip applies to his art. His success is a product of his long devotion to the study of comedy and to the perfection of his craft.

Not long after Flip had made up his mind to become a professional comedian, he visited a second-hand bookstore. There, he came across an old copy of **The Enjoyment of Laughter** by Max Eastman. The book contained a lengthy analysis of why people laugh. Like a student preparing for a final exam, Flip carefully studied the book's contents. "The book added a lot to my knowledge of myself, what about me was funny

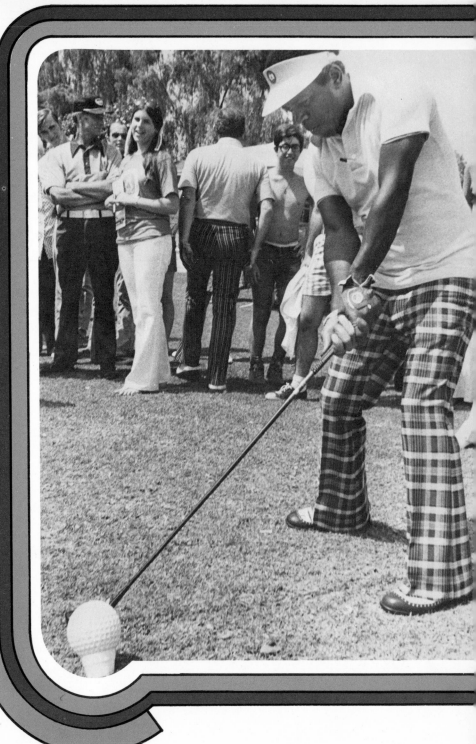

and why it was funny," Flip remembers. Soon the young comedian began gathering his own observations about laughter. He still keeps a notebook with the title, "Flip's Laws of Comedy." It contains several rules: "Things can be funny only when we are in fun. When we are in dead earnest, humor is the thing that is dead." Later he suggests, "Be unimpassioned — do not jest about things that matter too much."

Along with his own analysis of comedy, Flip studied the styles and techniques of other famous comedians. He discovered that each one had developed a quality which made him unique. Jack Benny was a master of comic timing. Like a song, Benny's stories depended on a rhythm. His punch-lines were delivered at precisely the right moment. Jerry Lewis depended on wild, physical energy. Groucho Marx and W. C. Fields always controlled the crazy situations they created. Flip decided that his own best quality was an ability to be casual and relaxed. His stories were funny because of his natural, cool delivery. "Be interesting," he wrote in his notebook, "Be effortless. To be effortless may require years of effort."

Flip's years of effort gradually produced a long list of famous stories and well-known characters, such as Reverend Leroy and Freddie the Playboy. His classic Christopher Columbus routine takes only 4 minutes to tell. Flip spent 3 years writing and re-working the story before it was ready for an audience.

His female character, Geraldine, also took years to develop. He borrowed her name from his boyhood girl-friend. Geraldine's voice came from two separate sources. Early in his career, during a brief stay in a small midwestern town, Flip watched a black soldier return to his family for the first time. The soldier's young sister stood at the door as the soldier approached. She turned to her mother and yelled, "Here come Willie back from the war, Mama. Show Mama how you can march, Willie, hup, two, three, four." A second source for Geraldine's voice was the movie, **Gone With the Wind.** In the film, Butterfly McQueen played the part of Prissy, a black maid. Prissy's voice had the same whiny, innocent quality that Flip wanted for his new character.

He borrowed the name and the voice, but Geraldine's appearance and her personality are Flip's own creations. He emphasizes that he has

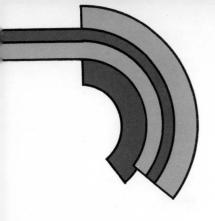

never intended Geraldine as an object of ridicule. On the contrary, he respects her. She was created as a comic compliment to the strength and endurance of black women. She may not be refined, but she is honest, outspoken and always in control. "She's liberated," smiles Flip, "she don't take no stuff."

During the four-year run of his television series, Flip devoted all of his creative energies to perfecting each program. Again, the cameras told a story of fresh, effortless fun, but off-camera, Flip kept a frantic schedule. No detail of the show's production was too minor for his attention. He had no time for nightclub appearances. He rarely took time to see a movie or go to a restaurant. He was almost never seen at Hollywood parties. Every day from 9 a.m. to 10 p.m., he worked with his producer, his director, his writers and the show's guests.

Each show took a full week of careful preparations. On Monday, Flip met with his production staff to read through the week's script. Long

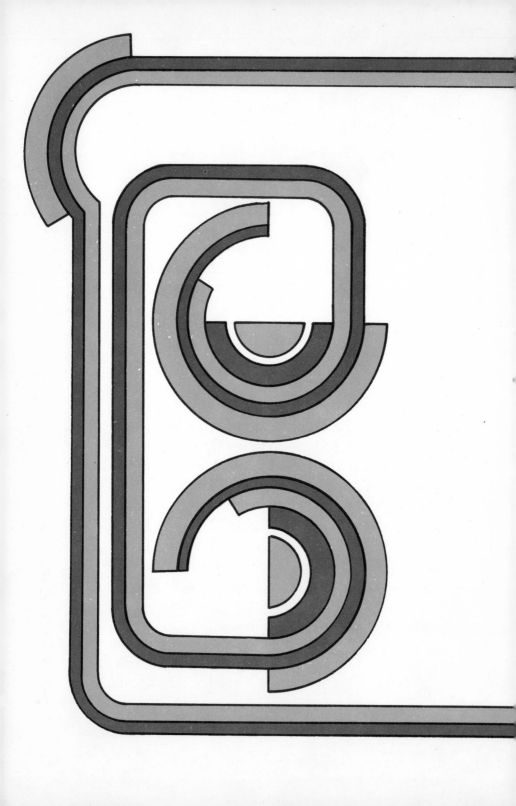

rehearsals consumed Tuesday and Wednesday. On Thursday, Flip and his guests worked all day with the camera crews. At 5 p.m. on Friday, the show was given a final dress-rehearsal, and, at 8 p.m. the same evening, the production was taped with a live studio audience.

Since the end of his weekly series in 1974, Flip has maintained a tight schedule. In addition to frequent guest appearances on television and four more "Flip Wilson Specials" for NBC, he has recently discovered golf. When time permits, Flip lends his newly developed athletic talent to numerous charity golf tournaments.

Next to golf, Flip's favorite release from the tensions of his production schedule is his bright blue Rolls Royce. He likes to escape into the California desert alone. Next to him on the front seat he keeps a pad of paper to record new ideas and new funny lines. He can't escape his constant drive to be funny.

Once upon a time, a small school boy pretended to be Clara Barton to help his school raise a little money for band uniforms. Times changed. The school boy grew up and one day someone offered him $86,000 a minute to sell soap on his television show.

Now, if you're Flip Wilson, that's really funny.